A bully can be a boy, a girl, or a group of kids.

A bully acts tough and hurts others by

pushing,

hitting,

teasing,

threatening,

name calling,

picking fights,

or doing other mean things.

A bully may push others around
because he doesn't know how to make friends
or because **he** was pushed around himself.

You can stand up for yourself
when a bully tries to boss you around
or threatens to hurt you.

You can stay calm,

stand tall,

and look the bully in the eyes.

You can also walk away or ask a grown-up for help.

What can you do if someone tells you
to get off the swing but it is still your turn?

You can be calm.
Look the person in the eyes
and say in a firm but kind voice,
"You need to wait your turn.
You can use the swing when my turn is over."

Why?

Because being calm and firm shows that
you can stand up for yourself
by not letting someone boss you around.

What can you do if someone teases you
about something that you are wearing?

You can be confident.
Smile and say, "I like what I am wearing,"
and then calmly walk away.

Why?

Because being confident shows that you can
stand up for yourself by being happy
with who you are and how you look.

What can you do if someone calls you names?

You can ignore the mean words and walk away.

Why?

Because ignoring the mean words and walking away
shows that you can stand up for yourself by not
getting upset when someone calls you names.

What can you do if someone says that
he is going to hurt you?

You can go ask a grown-up for help right away.
You should always get help
if someone is threatening to hurt you!

Why?

Because when you are in danger,
the best way to stand up for yourself
is to ask a grown-up for help.

What can you do if someone is mean to a classmate?